The Country Songbird Quilt

The

Country
Songbird
Quilt

Cheryl A. Benner
and
Rachel T. Pellman

also
"The Country Songbird Nine-Patch Variation Quilt"

Intercourse, PA 17534

Acknowledgments

Design by Cheryl A. Benner
Cover and color photography by Jonathan Charles
Author photo by Kenneth Pellman

The Country Songbird Quilt
© 1990 by Good Books, Intercourse, PA 17534
International Standard Book Number:
1-56148-006-1
Library of Congress Catalog Card Number:
90-71120

Library of Congress Cataloging-in-Publication Data

Benner, Cheryl A., 1962–
    The country songbird quilt: also, the country songbird nine-patch
variation quilt / Cheryl A. Benner and Rachel T. Pellman.
    p. 1   cm.

    1. Quilting—Patterns.   I. Pellman, Rachel T. (Rachel
Thomas) II. Title.
TT835.B353   1990   746.9′7—dc20   90-71120

ISBN 1-56148-006-1 (paperbk.) : $12.95

Table of Contents

The Country Songbird Quilt

Glorious springtime, resplendent with bright flowers and cheerful birds, is captured in the Country Songbird quilt design. Birds and tulips have long been favorite motifs for makers of applique quilts. The Country Songbird combines these elements, along with berries and clovers in a gentle winding wreath design.

The quilt top consists of five square patches, each set on an angle to allow for triangular shaped patches along the sides and at each corner. The center square is filled with an elaborately quilted bird cage. The door stands ajar and flowers climb the side of the open cage like a trellis. Surrounding the center patch are four appliqued patches. Each is filled with a wreath of flowers and berries. Two plump, fanciful birds alight on each wreath, their wings poised for flight. The remaining triangular patches are laced with applique tulips and clovers. The design on the pillow throw combines applique flowers and birds with a quilted cage. Bordering the bedcover is a series of quilted tulips and swirls, accented at each corner with additional applique work. The border may be further embellished by using applique tulips along the sides and bottom of the quilt. A scalloped edge follows the lines of the quilted border to finish the quilt with a flourish.

The Country Songbird has several assembly variations. It can be done using a fifth applique wreath patch in place of the quilted cage. Another option is to use nine square patches. In this variation the center and four corner patches are appliqued. Quilting fills the four alternate patches. Quilting lines echo the circular wreath design. Swirls, leaves and clovers, balanced with an elegant fan motif, encircle a series of chevron lines.

A single applique patch can be used to make coordinating pillows. One patch with a border makes a lovely wallhanging.

We present the Country Songbird in several colors and variations. Its possibilities are as varied as the individual quiltmakers who create them. Enjoy!

How to Begin

Read the following instructions thoroughly before beginning work on your quilt.

Wash all fabrics before cutting them. This process will both pre-shrink and test them for colorfastness. If the fabric is not colorfast after one washing, repeat the washings until the water remains clear or replace the cloth with another fabric. If fabrics are wrinkled after washing and drying, iron them before using them.

Fabrics suitable for quilting are generally lightweight, tightly woven cotton and cotton/polyester blends. They should not unravel easily and should not hold excessive wrinkles when squeezed and released. Because of the hours of time required to make a quilt, it is worth investing in high quality fabrics.

Fabric requirements given here are for standard 45″ wide fabric. If you use wider or more narrow fabrics, calculate the variations you will need.

All seams are sewn using ¼″ seam allowances. Measurements given include seam allowances except for applique pieces (see "How to Applique" section.)

Applique Quilts

Preparing Background Fabric

When purchasing fabric to be used for background and borders, it is best to buy the total amount needed from one bolt of fabric. This will assure that all the patches and borders will be the same shade. Dye lots can vary significantly from bolt to bolt of fabric, and those differences are emphasized when placed next to each other in a quilt top.

Cutting diagrams are shown to make the most efficient use of fabric. Label each piece after it is cut. Mark right and wrong sides of fabric as well.

So that you know where to place the applique pieces on the background piece, trace the applique design lightly on the right side of the background fabric before beginning to stitch. Even though the applique pieces will be laid over these markings and stitched in place, it is important to mark these lines as lightly as possible. Center the applique designs on the background sections. The placement of the applique on the pillow throw is an exception to that rule. Center that applique from side to side, but place it nearer the top of the quilt so that there is extra fullness for tucking the quilt under the pillows. The space from the top of the pillow-throw section to the highest point of the applique design should measure about 10 inches.

Making Templates

Make templates from pattern pieces printed in this book, using material that will not wear along the edges from repeated tracing. Cardboard is suitable for pieces being traced only a few times. Plastic lids or the sides of plastic cartons work well for templates that will be used repeatedly. Quilt supply shops and art supply stores carry sheets of plastic that work well for template-making.

Quiltmaking demands precision. Remember that as you begin marking. First, test the template you have made against the original printed pattern for accuracy. The applique templates are given in their actual size, without seam allowances. Trace them that way. Then trace them on the right side of the fabric, but spaced far enough apart so that you can cut them approximately ¼" outside the marked line. The traced line is the fold line indicating the exact shape of the applique piece. Since these lines will be on the right side of the fabric and will be on the folded edge, markings should be as light as possible.

Each applique piece needs to be traced separately (rather than having the fabric doubled) so the fold line is marked on each one. However, since some of the pieces face opposite directions, half should be traced one way and the other half should be traced the opposite way. (See illustration.)

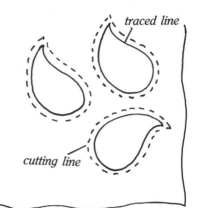

Applique templates should be traced on the right side of the fabric but spaced far enough apart so they can be cut approximately ¼" outside the marked line.

Appliqueing

Begin by appliqueing the cut-out fabric pieces, one at a time, over the placement lines drawn onto the background fabric pieces. Be alert to the sequence in which the pieces are applied, so that sections which overlay each other are done in proper order. In cases where a portion of an applique piece is covered by another, the section being covered does not need to be stitched, since it will be held in place by the stitches of the section that overlays it.

Appliqueing is not difficult, but it does require patience and precision. The best applique work has perfectly smooth curves and sharply defined points. To achieve this, stitches must be very small and tight. First, pin the piece being appliqued to the outline on the background piece. Using thread that matches the piece being applied, stitch the piece to the background section, folding the seam allowance under to the traced line on the applique piece. Fold under only a tiny section at a time.

The applique stitch is a running stitch going through the background fabric and emerging to catch only a few threads of the appliqued piece along the folded line. The needle should re-enter the background piece for the next stitch at almost the same place it emerged, creating a stitch so small that it is almost invisible along the edge of the appliqued piece. Stitches on the underside of the background fabric should be about ⅛" long.

To form sharp points, fold in one side and stitch almost to the end of the point. Fold in the opposite side to form the point and push the excess seam allowance under with the point of the needle. Excess seam allowance may be trimmed to eliminate bulk. Stitch tightly.

To form smooth curves, clip along the curves to the fold line. Fold under while stitching, using the needle to push under the seam allowances.

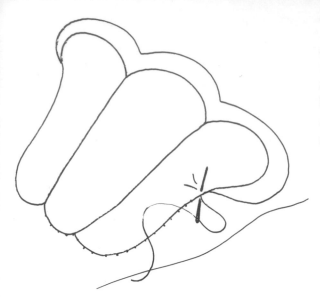

The applique stitch is a tiny, tight stitch that goes through the background fabric and emerges to catch only a few threads of the appliqued piece along the fold line.

Quilting lines are marked on the surface of the quilt top. Markings should be as light as possible so they are easily seen for quilting, yet do not distract when the quilting is completed.

Assembling the Appliqued Quilt Top

When all applique work is completed, the patches are ready to be assembled. See the diagram on page 13. Most applique work on the borders may be done before assembling the quilt top. However, the applique work on the corner will need to be completed after assemblage.

Quilting on Applique and Pieced Quilts

Marking Quilting Designs

Quilting designs are marked on the surface of the quilt top. A lead pencil provides a thin line and, if used with very little pressure, creates markings that are easily seen for quilting, yet do not distract when the quilt is completed. There are numerous marking pencils on the market, as well as chalk markers. Test whatever you choose on a scrap piece of fabric to be sure it performs as promised. Remember, quilting lines are not covered up by quilting stitches, so the lines should be light or removable.

Patterns for quilting designs are included in this book. Since most spread over several pages, you will need to assemble them before using them.

Quilting

A quilt consists of three layers—the back or underside of the quilt, the batting, and the top, which is the appliqued layer. Quilting stitches follow a decorative pattern, piercing through all three layers of the quilt "sandwich" and holding it together.

Many quilters prefer to stretch their quilts into large quilting frames. These are built so that the finished area of the quilt can be rolled up as work on it progresses. This type of frame allows space for several quilters to work on the same quilt and is used at quilting bees. Smaller hoops can be used to quilt small sections at a time. If you use one of the smaller frames, it is important that you first stretch the three layers of the quilt in the frame, then baste them securely together to prevent puckering.

The quilting stitch is a simple running stitch. Quilting needles are called "betweens" and are shorter than "sharps," which are regular handsewing needles. The higher the number, the smaller the needle. Many quilters prefer a size 8 or 9 needle.

Quilting is done with a single strand of quilting thread. Knot the thread and insert the needle through the top layer, about one inch away from the point where quilting should emerge on a marked quilting line. Gently tug the knot through the fabric so it is hidden between the layers. Then bring the needle up through the quilt top, going through all layers of the quilt.

Keep one hand under the quilt to feel when the needle has successfully penetrated all layers and to help guide the needle back up to the surface. Your upper hand receives the needle and repeats the process. It is possible to stack as many as five stitches on the needle before pulling the thread through. However, when you work curves, you have smoother results if you stack fewer stitches. Pull the quilting stitches taut but not so tight as to pucker the fabric. When you have used the entire length of thread, reinforce the stitching with a tiny backstitch. Then reinsert the needle in the top layer, push it through for a long stitch, pull it out and clip it.

The goal in quilting is to have straight, even stitches that are of equal length on both the top and bottom of the quilt. That achievement comes with hours of practice.

When you quilt the applique patches, simply outline the applique designs. This outline quilting will accent the applique section and cause it to appear slightly puffed.

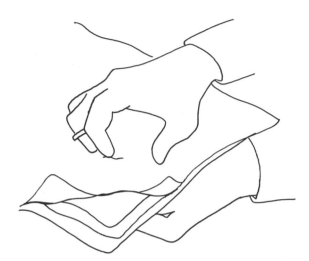

A quilt is a sandwich of three layers—the quilt back, batting and the quilt top—all held together by the quilting stitches.

Binding

The final stage in completing a quilt is the binding, which finishes the quilt's raw edge. When binding a non-straight-edged quilt, cut the binding strips on the bias. This allows more flex and stretch around curves. To cut on the bias, cut the fabric at a 45 degree angle to the straight of grain.

A double thickness of binding on the edge of the quilt gives it additional strength and durability. To create a double binding, cut the binding strips 2–2½" wide. Sew strips together to form a continuous length of binding.

When binding a quilt with scalloped edges, it is easier to attach the binding before cutting the scalloped edge. To do so, baste the raw edges of the quilt together. Mark but do not cut the scalloped border. Using a ¼" seam allowance, sew the binding along the marked edge. Trim the scallops even with the edge of the binding. Wrap the binding around to the back, enclosing the raw edges and covering the stitch line. Slipstitch in place with thread that matches the color of the binding fabric.

To Display Quilts

Wall quilts can be hung in various ways. You can simply tack the quilt directly to the wall. However, this is potentially damaging to both the quilt and wall. Except for a permanent hanging, this is probably not the best way.

Another option is to hang the quilt like a painting. To do this, make a narrow sleeve from matching fabric and handsew it to the upper edge of the quilt along the back. Insert a dowel rod through the sleeve and hang the rod by wire or nylon string.

The quilt can also be hung on a frame. This method requires velcro or fabric to be attached to the frame itself. If you choose velcro, staple one side to the frame. Handsew the opposite velcro on the edge of the quilt, then attach the quilt carefully to the velcro on

Mitering Corners

Step 1

Measure in from each end the exact number of inches as the border width. Draw a diagonal line from that point to the outer corner. Cut along angled line.

Step 2

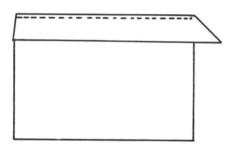

Stitch borders to quilt, leaving a ¼" seam allowance open at each mitered end.

Step 3

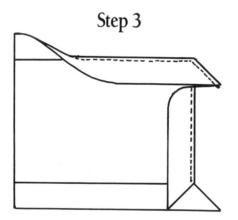

Stitch across the open ends of the corners from the inside corner to the outer edge.

the frame. If you attach fabric to the frame, handstitch the quilt to the frame itself.

Quilts can also be mounted inside plexiglas by a professional framery. This method, often reserved for antique quilts, can provide an acid-free, dirt-free and, with special plexiglas, a sun-proof environment for your quilt.

Other Projects

The Country Songbird pattern is adaptable to other projects as well. To make a wallhanging, follow the instructions for appliqueing but use only one square patch. This may be done as a single square like the patches of the Country Songbird Variation. Add a border with decorative quilting and you have a lovely wallhanging. For a longer wallhanging, tip the square patch on an angle as in the original design. Add a triangle with applique flowers on each corner to create a square. Surround this with a border and bind with a scalloped edge or a straight edge. Borders on wallhangings may be mitered for a more tailored look. See illustration for instructions on mitered corners.

Pillows can also be made using a single patch. Applique the pillow top and quilt the patch. To make the back of the pillow, cut a square equal in size to the front in either matching or contrasting fabric.

Make a ruffle using one of the fabrics used in the applique design. To make the ruffle, cut three strips of fabric measuring 4½" x 45" each. Sew these strips together to form a continuous length. Bring the two ends together, wrong sides together, and stitch to create a fabric circle. Fold the fabric circle in half with wrong sides together. Stitch along the raw edge with a long running stitch the entire circumference of the circle. Gather the circle to fit around the edges of the quilted top. Pin the ruffle to the pillow top with the raw edges even and spread the gathers evenly throughout. Baste ruffle to pillow top.

With right sides together and ruffle sandwiched between the layers, pin back to pillow top. Stitch back to top through all layers, leaving a five-inch opening along one side. Trim seams. Turn pillow right side out. Stuff pillow with polyester fiberfil. Slipstitch opening.

Signing and Dating Quilts

To preserve history for future generations, sign and date the quilts you make. Include your initials and the year the quilt was made. This date is usually added discreetly in a corner of the quilt. It can be embroidered or quilted among the quilting designs. Another alternative is to stitch or write the information on a separate piece of fabric and handstitch it to the back of the quilt. Whatever method you choose, this is an important part of finishing a quilt.

The Country Songbird Quilt
Cutting Lay-out for Queen-size or Double-size Quilt

Final size—approximately 93″ × 108″
Measurements include seam allowances

Total yardage for quilt top—8⅜ yards
Total yardage for quilt back—6¼ yards
plus 11″ remaining from cutting
borders of quilt top.

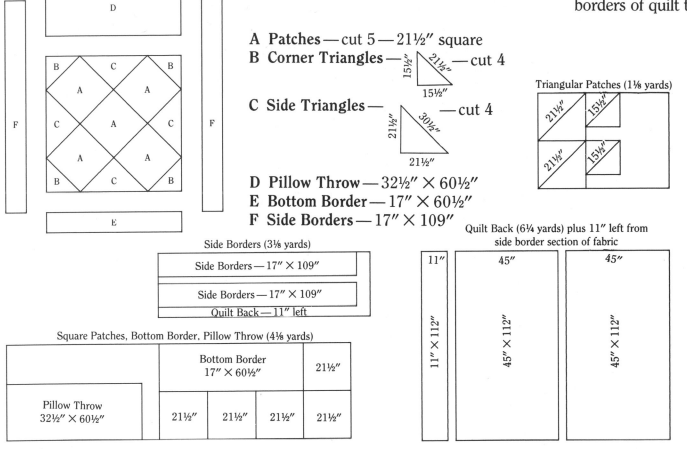

A Patches—cut 5—21½″ square
B Corner Triangles—15½″ 21½″ 15½″—cut 4

C Side Triangles—21½″ 30½″ 21½″—cut 4

D Pillow Throw—32½″ × 60½″
E Bottom Border—17″ × 60½″
F Side Borders—17″ × 109″

Triangular Patches (1⅛ yards)
21½″ 15½″
21½″ 15½″

Side Borders (3⅛ yards)
Side Borders—17″ × 109″
Side Borders—17″ × 109″
Quilt Back—11″ left

Quilt Back (6¼ yards) plus 11″ left from
side border section of fabric
11″ 45″ 45″
11″ × 112″ 45″ × 112″ 45″ × 112″

Square Patches, Bottom Border, Pillow Throw (4⅛ yards)
Pillow Throw 32½″ × 60½″
Bottom Border 17″ × 60½″
21½″
21½″ 21½″ 21½″ 21½″

Assembly Instructions for the Country Songbird Quilt
Queen-size/Double-size

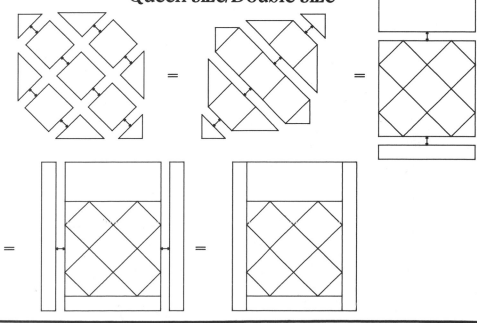

Fabric Requirements for Applique Pieces for the Country Songbird Quilt and the Country Songbird Quilt without the birdcage.

Large Birds—½ yd.
Large Bird Wing A—⅛ yd.
Large Bird Wing B—1/16 yd.
Small Birds—½ yd.
Small Bird Wing A—⅛ yd.
Small Bird Wing B—1/16 yd.
Back Panel of Tulip—¾ yd.

Front Panel of Tulip—¼ yd.
Top of Tulip—⅜ yd.
Rosebuds—⅛ yd.
Rosebud base—⅛ yd.
Clover—⅛ yd.
Leaves—1¼ yd. print
    1¼ yd. solid

Note: Bias tape is used for stems and clover accents. Embroidery floss is used for bird beaks and eyes. If tulips are appliqued on the border the following additional fabric is required:

Back Panel of Tulip—½ yd.
Front Panel of Tulip—¼ yd.
Top of Tulip—⅛ yd.
Leaves—⅜ yd. print
    ⅜ yd. solid

Fabric Requirements for Applique Pieces for the Country Songbird Nine-Patch Variation Quilt

Large Birds—½ yd.
Large Bird Wing A—⅛ yd.
Large Bird Wing B—1/16 yd.
Small Birds—½ yd.
Small Bird Wing A—⅛ yd.
Small Bird Wing B—1/16 yd.
Back Panel of Tulip—½ yd.

Front Panel of Tulip—⅛ yd.
Top of Tulip—¼ yd.
Rosebuds—⅛ yd.
Rosebud base—⅛ yd.
Clover—⅛ yd.
Leaves—¾ yd. print
    ¾ yd. solid

Country Songbird Quilt Applique Templates

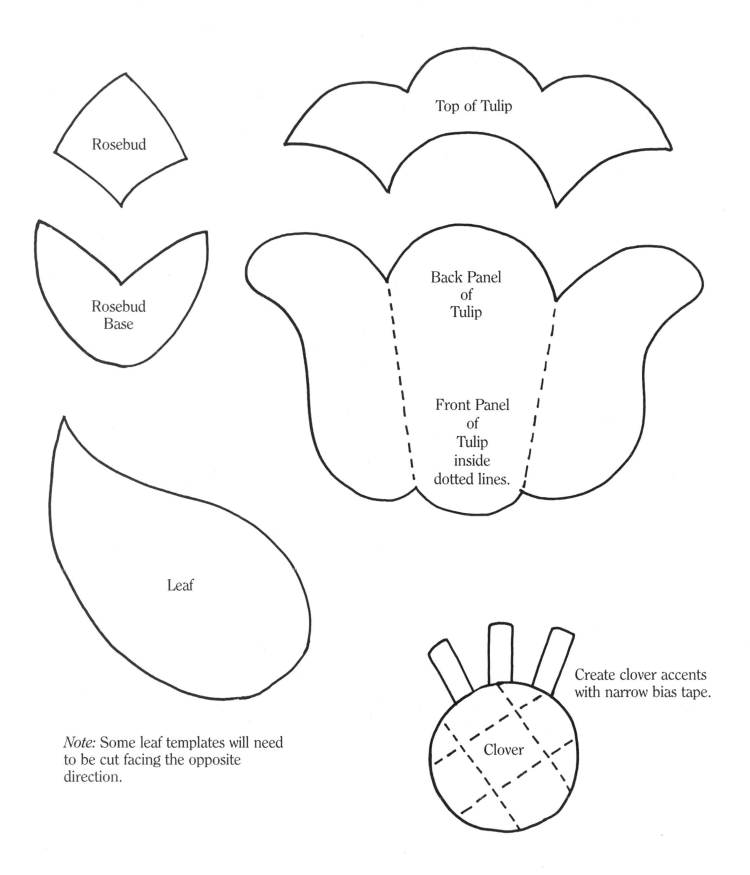

Rosebud

Top of Tulip

Rosebud Base

Back Panel of Tulip

Front Panel of Tulip inside dotted lines.

Leaf

Create clover accents with narrow bias tape.

Clover

Note: Some leaf templates will need to be cut facing the opposite direction.

Country Songbird Quilt Applique Templates

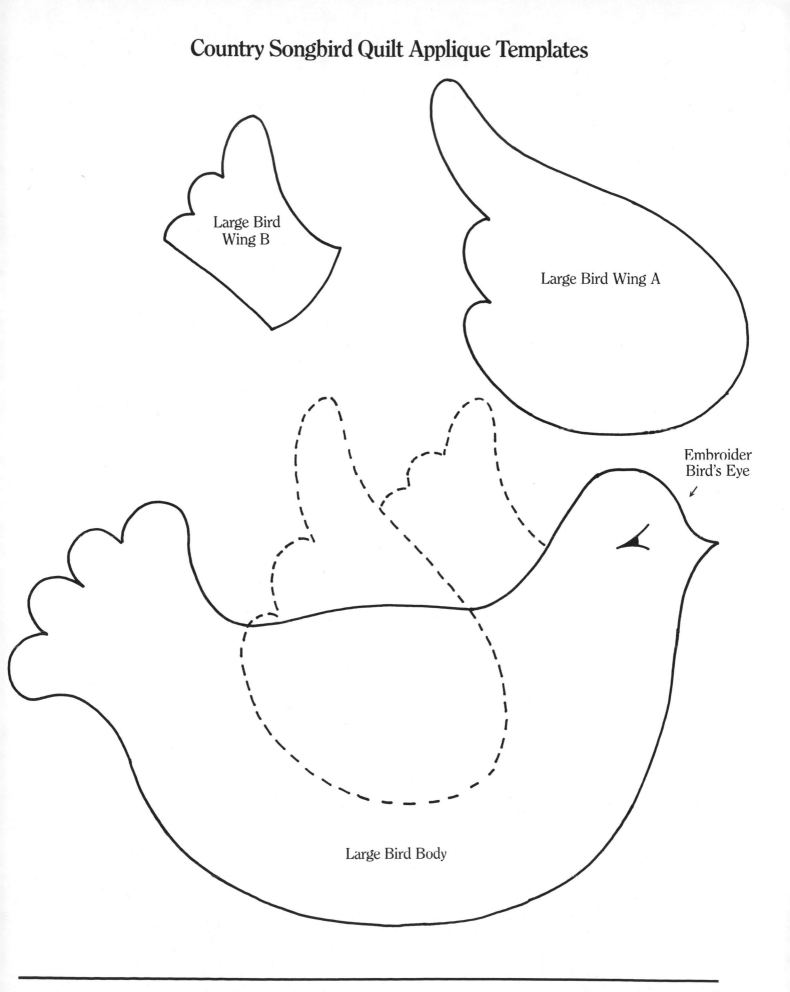

Large Bird
Wing B

Large Bird Wing A

Embroider
Bird's Eye

Large Bird Body

Country Songbird Quilt Applique Templates

Small Bird Wing B

Small Bird Wing A

Embroider Bird's Eye →

Small Bird Body

Country Songbird Quilt Applique Layout
Songbird Patch

Connect corresponding letters and notches along dotted lines and tape.

Completed layout will look like this:

Trim along dotted line.

Use narrow bias tape to create stems.

A

B

C

D

Trim along dotted line.

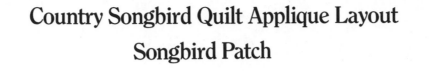

E

F

H

G

Trim along dotted line.

Trim along dotted line.

Country Songbird Quilt — Applique Layout
Songbird Patch

H

G

Trim along dotted line.

I

J

K

Trim along dotted line.

Country Songbird Quilt Applique Layout
Songbird Patch

Trim along dotted line.

Trim along dotted line.

Trim along dotted line.

I

J

K

L

M

Country Songbird Quilt Applique Layout
Songbird Patch

Trim along dotted line.

Trim along dotted line.

C

D

L

M

Country Songbird Quilt Applique Layout

Small Floral Triangle Patch

B

A

Trim along dotted line.

Connect corresponding letters and notches along dotted lines and tape.

Completed layout will look like this:

Dotted lines indicate quilting.

Trim along dotted line.

B

A

Country Songbird Quilt Applique Layout
Side Floral Triangle Patch

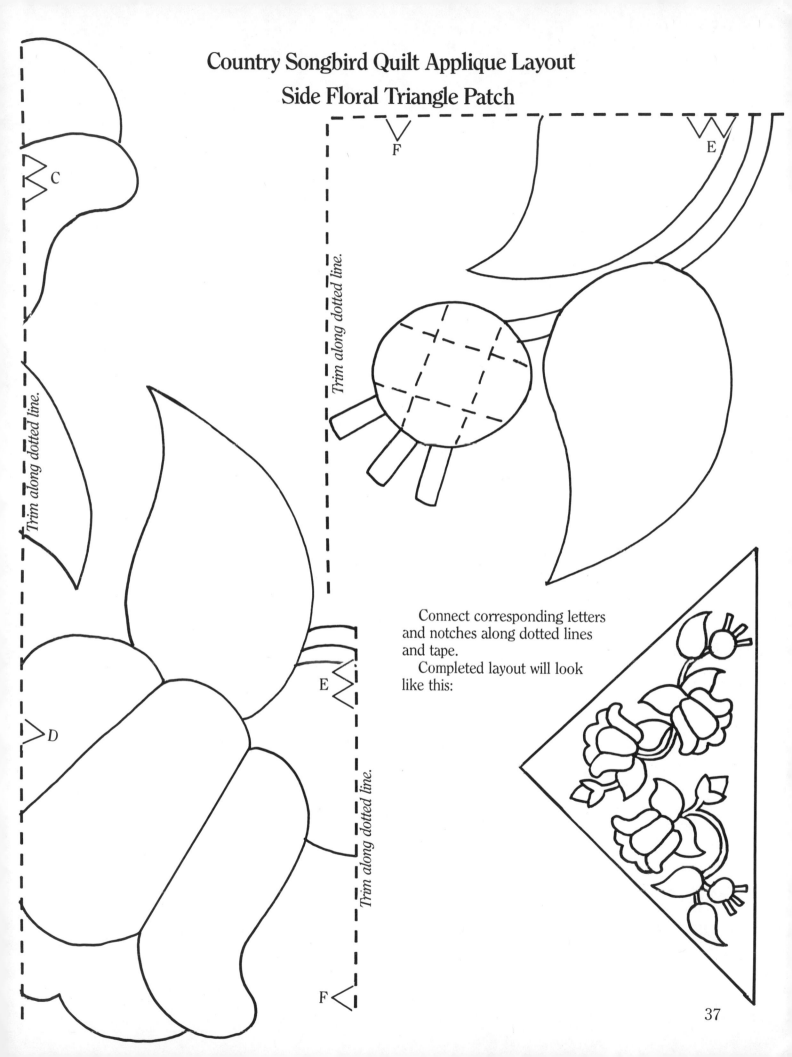

Trim along dotted line.

C

Trim along dotted line.

F

E

D

E

F

Connect corresponding letters and notches along dotted lines and tape.

Completed layout will look like this:

Trim along dotted line.

37

Country Songbird Quilt Applique Layout
Side Floral Triangle Patch

Trim along dotted line.

A

Trim along dotted line.

C

Use narrow bias tape to create stems.

D

B

39

Country Songbird Quilt Applique Layout
Side Floral Triangle Patch

A

Trim along dotted line.

B

Use narrow bias tape to create stems.

Dotted lines indicate quilting.

Country Songbird Quilt Quilting Template
Center Birdcage Patch

To create the quilted center Bird-cage patch template, match corresponding letters and notches along dotted lines and tape.

Completed template will look like this:

Trim along dotted line.

K

L

N

M

Trim along dotted line.

Country Songbird Quilt Quilting Template
Center Birdcage Patch

Trim along dotted line.

A

B

C

D

Trim along dotted line.

Country Songbird Quilt Quilting Template

Center Birdcage Patch

Trim along dotted line.

Trim along dotted line.

Country Songbird Quilt Quilting Template
Center Birdcage Patch

Trim along dotted line.

Trim along dotted line.

Country Songbird Quilt Applique Layout
Pillow Throw

Connect corresponding letters
and notches along dotted lines
and tape.
Completed layout will look
like this:

Trim along dotted line.

Country Songbird Quilt Applique
Pillow Throw

Layout

Birdcage is quilted.

B

A

C

D

Trim along dotted line.

Trim along dotted line.

Trim along dotted line.

Country Songbird Quilt Applique Layout
Pillow Throw

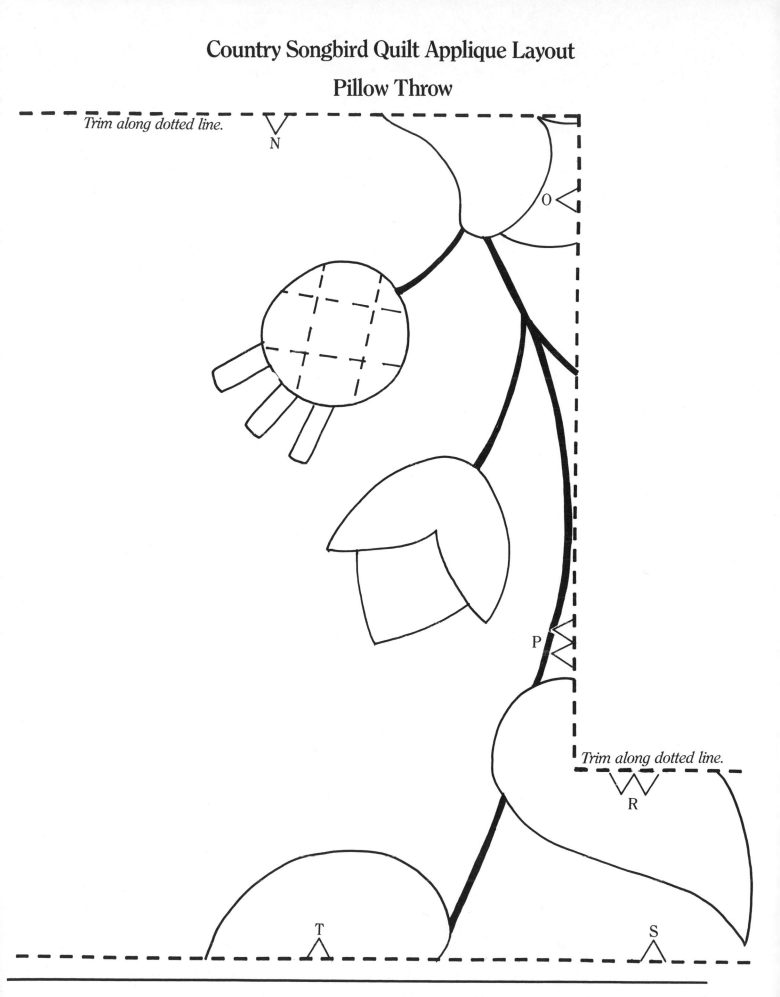

Country Songbird Quilt Applique Layout
Pillow Throw

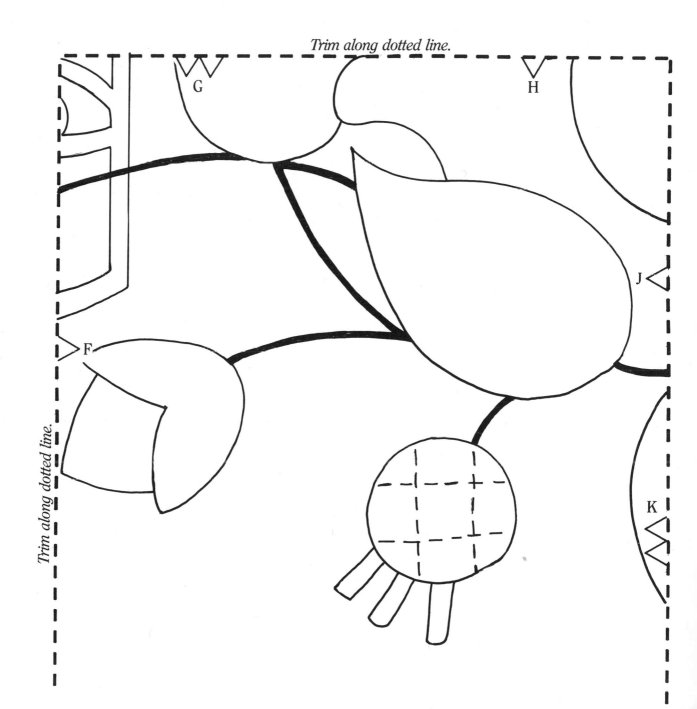

Trim along dotted line.

Trim along dotted line.

Country Songbird Quilt Applique Layout
Pillow Throw

Trim along dotted line.

Country Songbird Quilt Quilting Template
Pillow Throw Border of Swirls

Trim along dotted line.

A

B

Continue this border of swirls
along the base of the Pillow Throw
section.

A

B

Trim along dotted line.

Country Songbird Quilt Quilting Template
Scallop Border

Connect corresponding letters
and notches along dotted lines
and tape.
Completed layout will look
like this:

Use narrow bias tape to create stems.

Trim along dotted line.

G

H

I

J

K

L

Trim along dotted line.

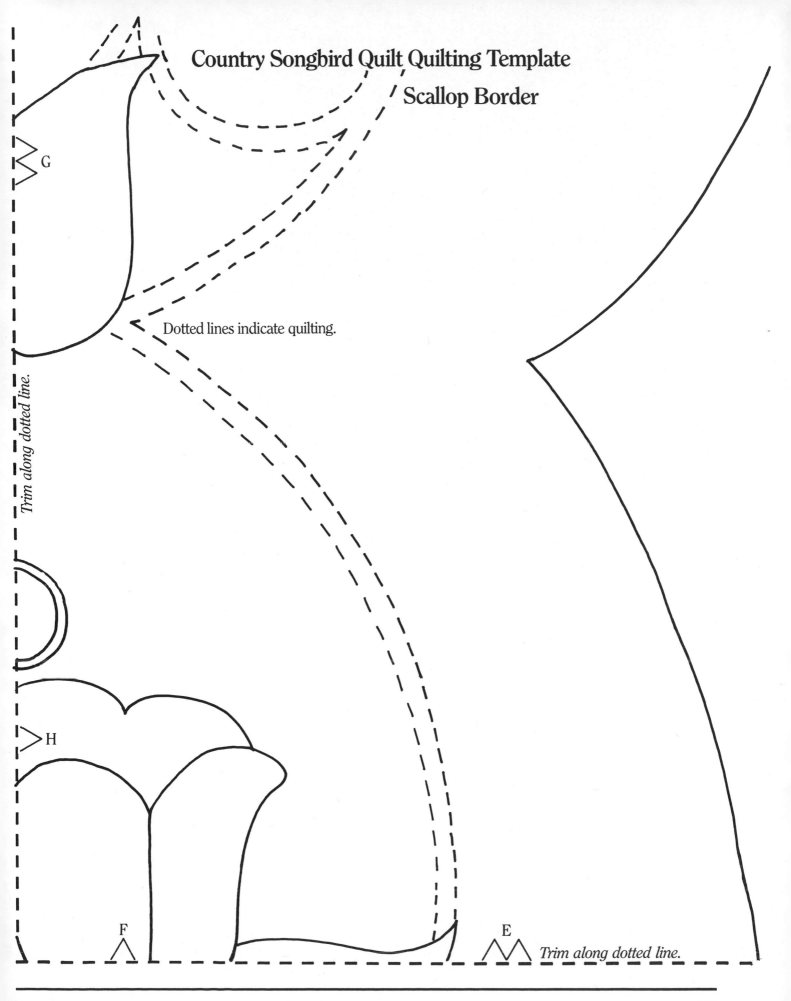

Country Songbird Quilt Quilting Template
Scallop Border

G

Trim along dotted line.

Dotted lines indicate quilting.

H

F

E

Trim along dotted line.

Country Songbird Quilt Quilting Template

Scallop Border

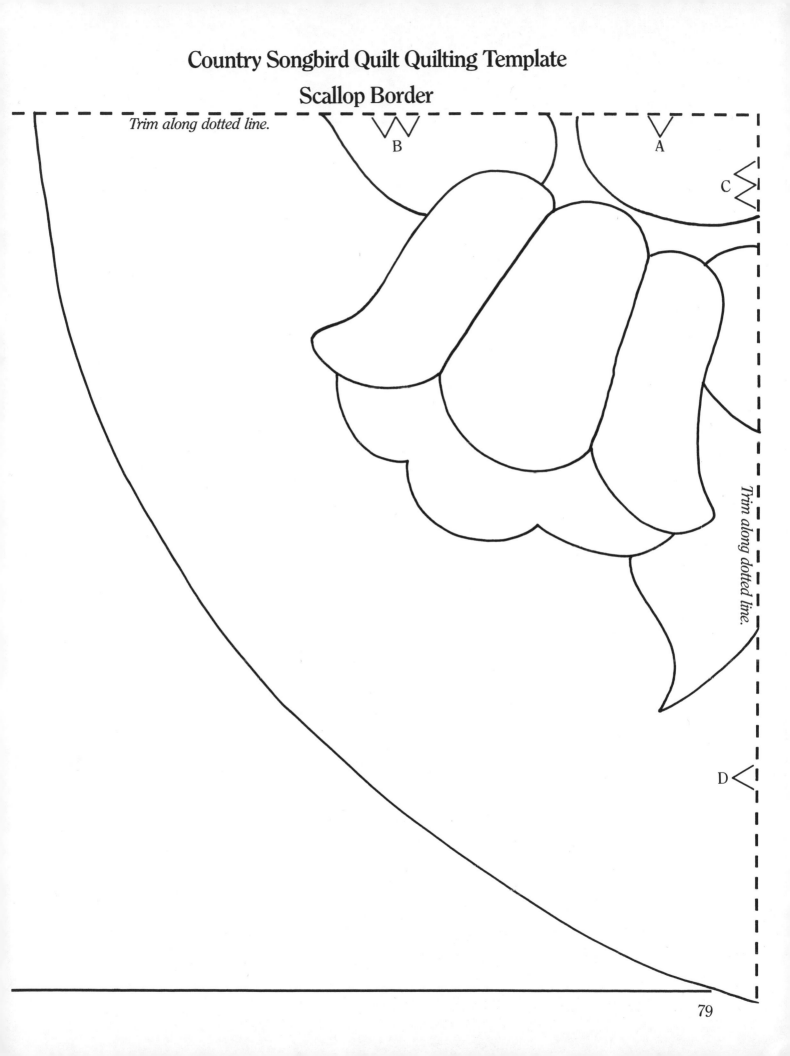

Trim along dotted line.

B

A

C

Trim along dotted line.

D

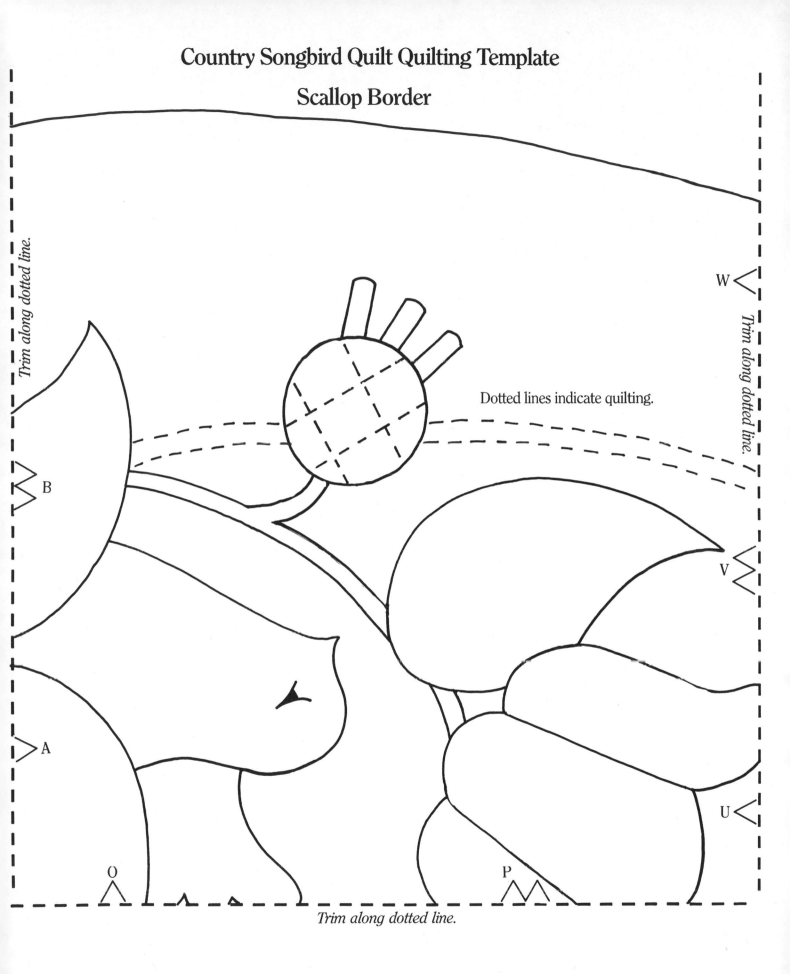

Trim along dotted line.

Trim along dotted line.

Dotted lines indicate quilting.

W

B

V

A

U

O

P

Trim along dotted line.

Country Songbird Quilt Quilting Template
Scallop Border

Trim along dotted line.

Trim along dotted line.

Trim along dotted line.

Country Songbird Quilt Quilting Template

Scallop Border

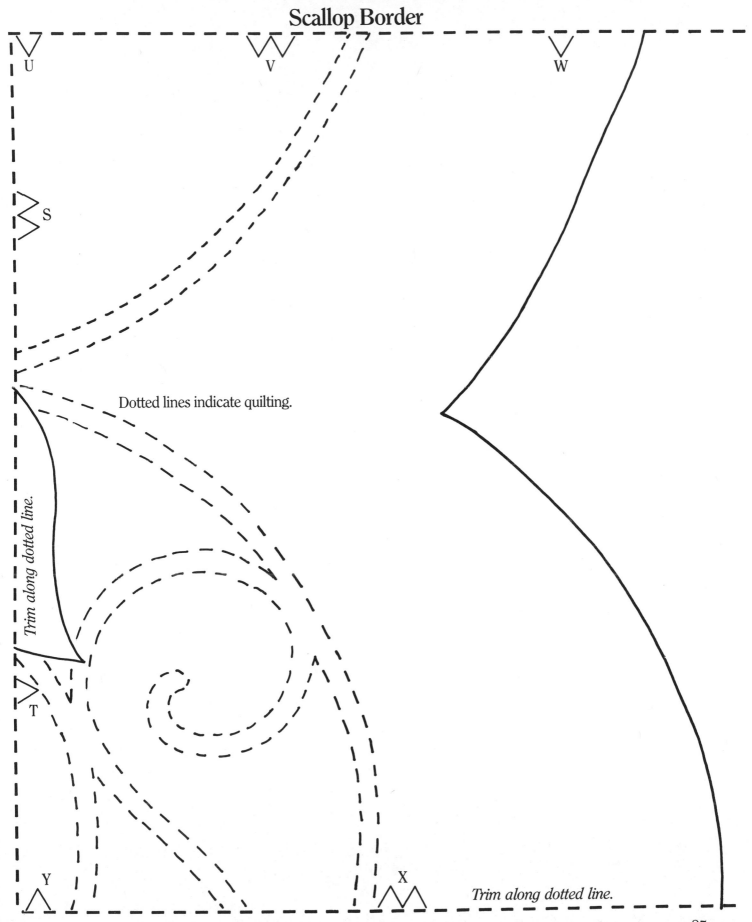

Dotted lines indicate quilting.

U

S

Trim along dotted line.

T

Y

X

Trim along dotted line.

V

W

Country Songbird Quilt Quilting Template

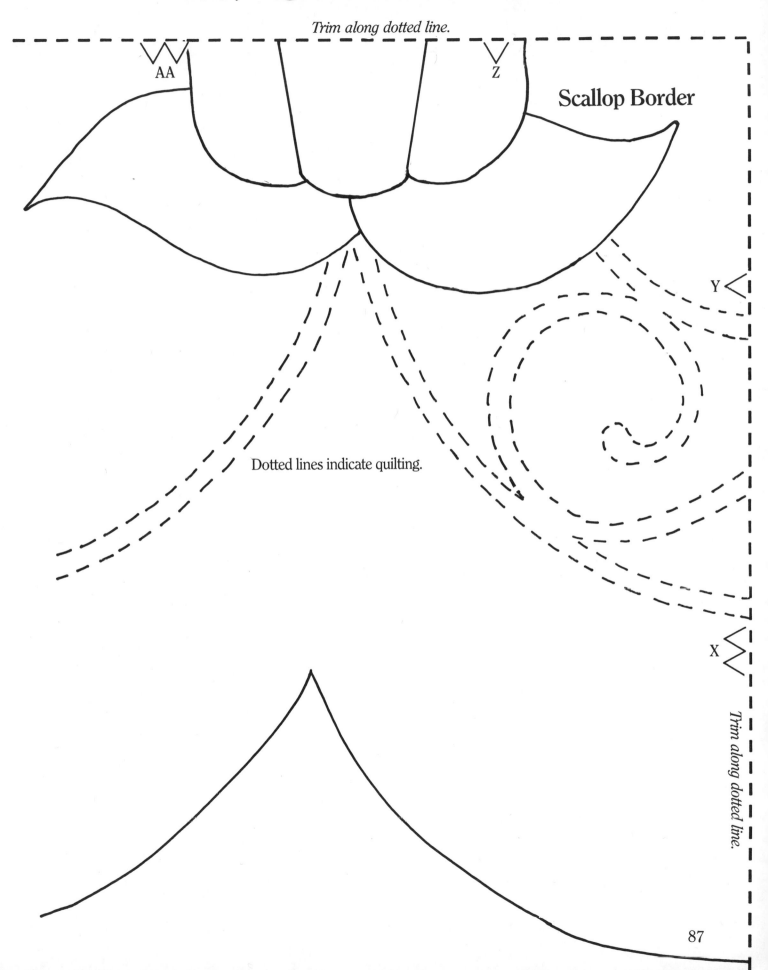

Scallop Border

AA

Z

Dotted lines indicate quilting.

Y

X

Country Songbird Quilt Quilting Template
Scallop Border

Trim along dotted line.

Trim along dotted line.

Trim along dotted line.

Trim along dotted line.

The Country Songbird Nine-Patch Variation Quilt

The Country Songbird Nine-Patch Variation Quilt
Cutting Lay-out for Queen-size or Double-size Quilt

Final size—approximately 96″ x 112″
Measurements include seam allowances

Total yardage for quilt top—9¼ yards
Total yardage for quilt back—6¼ yards
plus 11″ remaining from cutting borders of quilt top.

A Patches—cut 9—21½″ square
B Pillow Throw—33″ x 63½″
C Bottom Border—17″ x 63½″
D Side Borders—17″ x 112½″

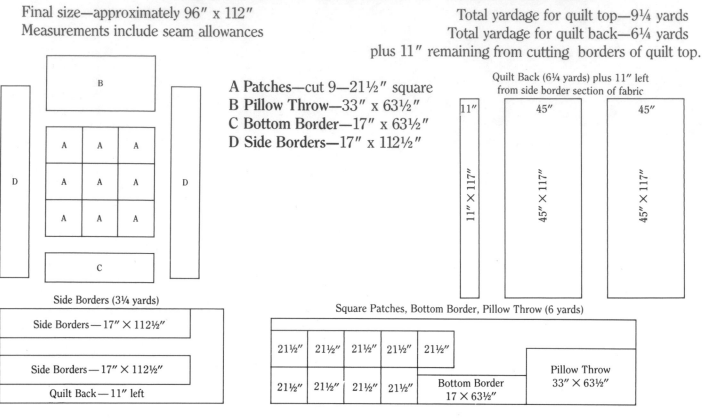

Side Borders (3¼ yards)

Side Borders—17″ × 112½″

Side Borders—17″ × 112½″

Quilt Back—11″ left

Quilt Back (6¼ yards) plus 11″ left from side border section of fabric

Square Patches, Bottom Border, Pillow Throw (6 yards)

| 21½″ | 21½″ | 21½″ | 21½″ | 21½″ | |
| 21½″ | 21½″ | 21½″ | 21½″ | Bottom Border 17 × 63½″ | Pillow Throw 33″ × 63½″ |

Assembly Instructions for the Country Songbird Nine-Patch Variation Quilt Queen-size/Double-size

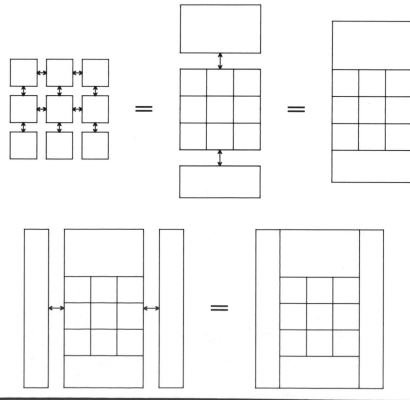

Country Songbird Quilt Quilting Template

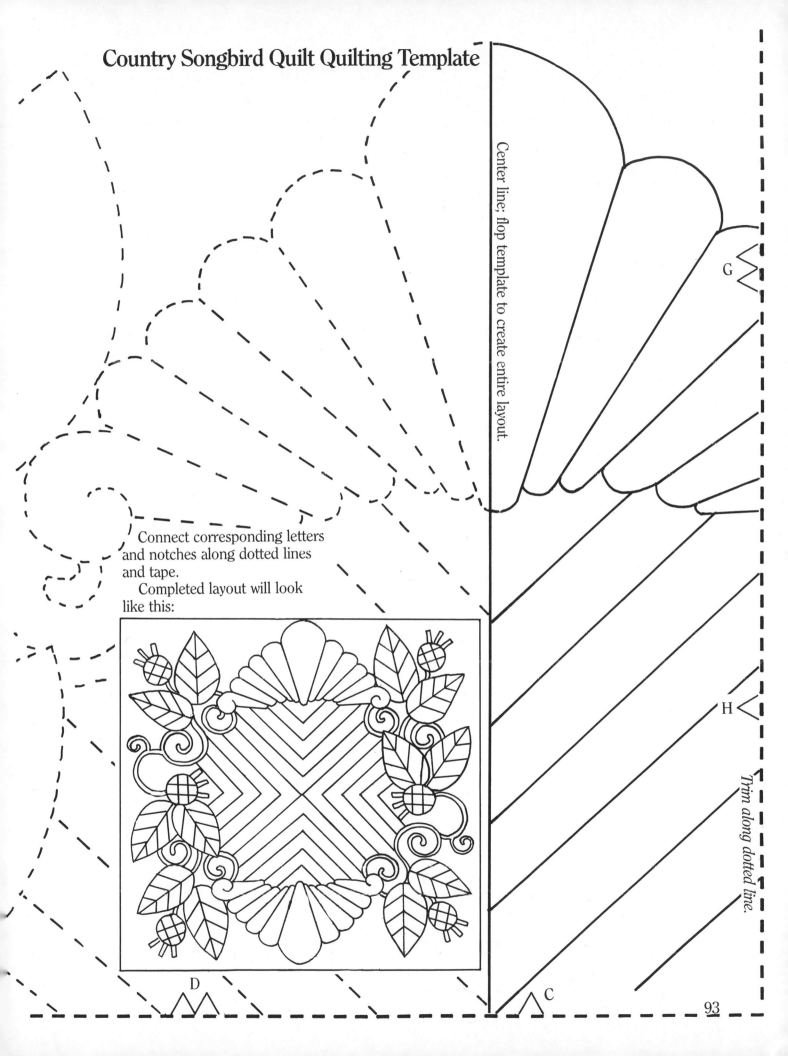

Center line; flop template to create entire layout.

Connect corresponding letters and notches along dotted lines and tape.

Completed layout will look like this:

G

H

D

C

Trim along dotted line.

Country Songbird Quilt Quilting Template

Trim along dotted line.

Country Songbird Quilt Quilting Template

Trim along dotted line.

E

A

B

F

Country Songbird Quilt Quilting Template

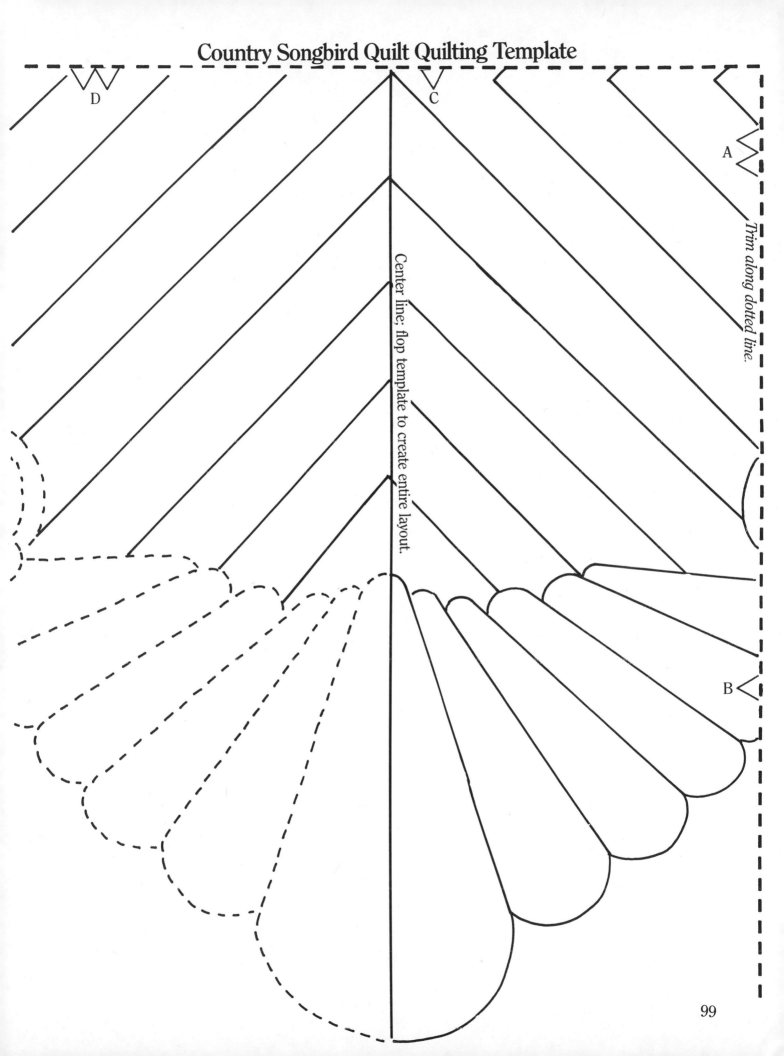

D

C

A

Trim along dotted line.

Center line; flop template to create entire layout.

B

Order Form

(all books are paperback)

<u>Quantity</u>

_____ copies of *The Country Songbird Quilt* @ $12.95 each = $ _____

_____ copies of *The Country Lily Quilt* @ $12.95 each = $ _____

_____ copies of *The Country Love Quilt* @ $12.95 each = $ _____

_____ copies of *The Country Bride Quilt* @ $12.95 each = $ _____

_____ copies of *Amish Quilt Patterns* @ $12.95 each = $ _____

_____ copies of *Small Amish Quilt Patterns* @ $10.95 each = $ _____

_____ copies of *Making Animal Quilts: Patterns and Projects* @ $10.95 each = $ _____

_____ copies of *Patterns for Making Amish Dolls and Doll Clothes* @ $12.95 each = $ _____

Subtotal $ _____

PA residents add 6% sales tax   _____

Shipping and handling (Add 5%, $1.50 minimum)   _____

TOTAL $ _____

METHOD OF PAYMENT

☐ Check or Money Order (payable to Good Books in U.S. funds)

☐ Please charge my:

     ☐ MasterCard   ☐ Visa

\# _____ _____ _____ _____ exp. date _____

Signature _____

Name _____

Name _____

Address _____

City _____ State ____ Zip _____

Telephone (_____) _____

SHIP TO: (if different)

Name _____

Address _____

City _____ State ____ Zip _____

Telephone (_____) _____

Mail order to **Good Books**, Main Street, Intercourse, PA 17534; Or call 1-800-762-7171 (in PA and Canada, call collect 717/768-7171).

(Prices subject to change without notice.)

About The Old Country Store

The People's Place Quilt Museum

Cheryl A. Benner and Rachel T. Pellman are on the staff of The old Country Store, located along Route 340 in Intercourse, Pennsylvania. The store offers crafts from more than 300 artisans, most of whom are local Amish and Mennonites. There are quilts of traditional and contemporary designs, patchwork pillows and pillow kits, afghans, stuffed animals, dolls, tablecloths and Christmas tree ornaments. Other handcrafted items include potholders, sunbonnets and wooden toys.

For the do-it-yourself quilter, the Store offers quilt supplies, fabric at discount prices, and a large selection of quilt books and patterns.

Located on the second floor of the Store is The People's Place Quilt Museum. The Museum, which opened in 1988, features antique Amish quilts and crib quilts as well as a small collection of dolls, doll quilts, socks and other decorative arts.

About The Authors

Cheryl A. Benner and Rachel T. Pellman together developed The Country Songbird Quilt and The Country Songbird Nine-Patch Variation Quilt. They designed the patterns, then selected fabrics and supervised the making of the original quilts by Lancaster County Mennonite women. This is Benner's and Pellman's third collaboration on a quilt design and book. Their earlier books were the popular *The Country Love Quilt* and *The Country Lily Quilt*.

Benner, her husband Lamar, and young son live in Honeybrook, Pa. She is a graduate of the Art Institute of Philadelphia (Pa.). Benner is art director for Good Enterprises, Intercourse, Pa.

Pellman lives in Lancaster, Pa., and is manager of The Old Country Store, Intercourse. She is co-author of *The Country Bride Quilt*.

She is the author of *Amish Quilt Patterns* and *Small Amish Quilt Patterns;* co-author with Jan Steffy of *Patterns for Making Amish Dolls and Doll Clothes;* and co-author with her husband, Kenneth, of *The World of Amish Quilts, Amish Crib Quilts,* and *Amish Doll Quilts, Dolls, and Other Playthings.*

The Pellmans are the parents of two sons.